THE COMPLETE PIANO PLAYER
BOOK 4

W9-BHB-923

'By the end of this book your playing will
be even more colourful and varied,
and you will be playing 22 popular songs,
including: *Don't Cry For Me Argentina,*
Just The Way You Are,
The Sound Of Silence, and *My Way.*'

Kenneth Baker

Wise Publications
London/New York/Paris/Sydney/Copenhagen/Madrid

Exclusive Distributors:
Music Sales Limited
8/9 Frith Street, London W1V 5TZ, England.
Music Sales Pty Limited
120 Rothschild Avenue, Rosebery, NSW 2018, Australia.

This book © Copyright 1984, 1993 by
Wise Publications
ISBN 0-7119-0434-0
UK Order No. AM34851

Book designed by Howard Brown
Book photography by Peter Wood

Music Sales' complete catalogue lists thousands of
titles and is free from your local music shop, or direct from Music Sales Limited.
Please send a cheque/postal order for £1.50 for postage to:
Music Sales Limited, Newmarket Road, Bury St. Edmunds,
Suffolk IP33 3YB.

Printed in the United Kingdom by
Halstan & Co Limited, Amersham, Buckinghamshire.

Your Guarantee of Quality
As publishers, we strive to produce every book to the
highest commercial standards.
The music has been freshly engraved and the book has been
carefully designed to minimise awkward page turns
and to make playing from it a real pleasure.
Particular care has been given to specifying acid-free,
neutral-sized paper made from pulps which have not been elemental chlorine bleached.
This pulp is from farmed sustainable forests and was produced with special
regard for the environment.
Throughout, the printing and binding have been planned to ensure a sturdy,
attractive publication which should give years of enjoyment.
If your copy fails to meet our high standards, please inform us
and we will gladly replace it.

Morning

Edvard Grieg

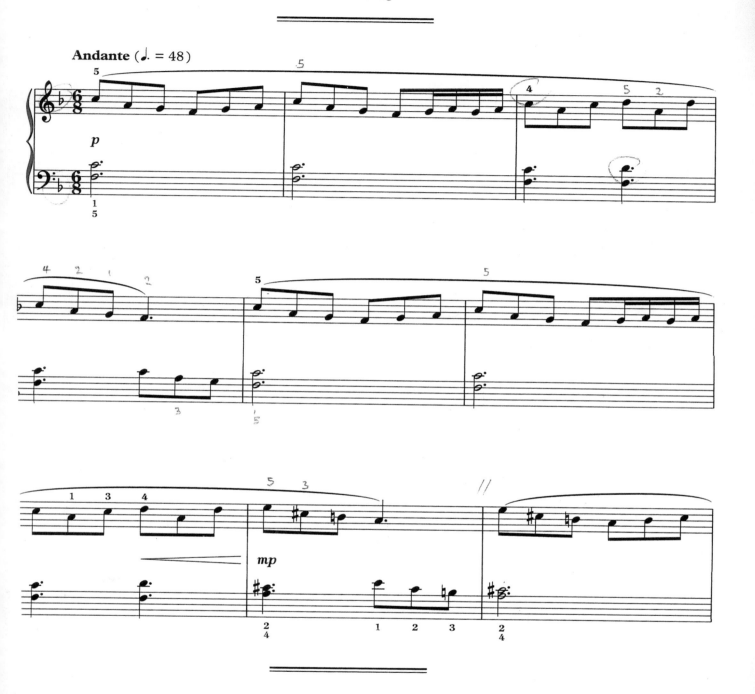

Morning is the first movement of a suite of pieces by the Norwegian composer Edvard Grieg (1843–1907). The suite was written as incidental music to Ibsen's play *Peer Gynt* and also contains the famous *In The Hall Of The Mountain King*.

Pay careful attention to the phrasing in this piece. Keep the quavers even and controlled and don't rush the semiquavers – they are not as fast as they look! Notice how the dynamics gradually build up through the piece until the loudest point at bar 21.

CONTENTS

About this book, 5

ABOUT THIS BOOK

Book Four takes you a giant step along your road to becoming the complete piano player.

It introduces you to the piano pedals, and you will be delighted at how much colour the Sustaining Pedal will add to your playing.

Your study of 'syncopation' begins here too, and you will learn several great syncopated numbers guaranteed to set the foot tapping.

Because it is important, for the sake of contrast, to play in a number of different keys, you will learn five new ones–including three 'minor' keys.

There are also some new piano techniques which will improve your playing, such as playing in octaves with the right hand, and 'filling in' with the left hand.

As usual all lessons are based on well known songs made famous by great artists, or tuneful classical compositions. By the end of the book you will have twenty-two exciting new solos to add to your repertoire.

FIVE NEW NOTES FOR LEFT HAND

Here are some important new notes for you to learn:

Low C, D and E
High F and F Sharp

All for left hand

C D E

F   F♯

THE TOUCH OF YOUR LIPS

Words & Music: Ray Noble

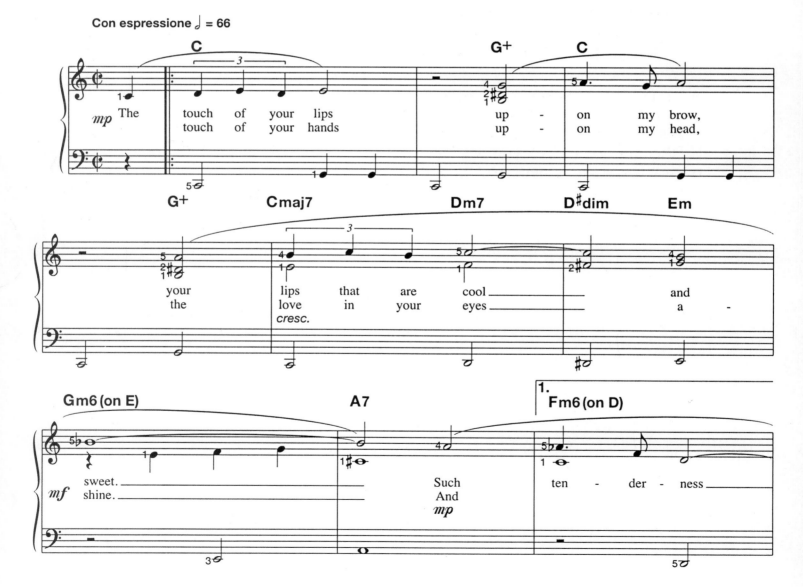

Look out for the new left hand low notes in the following piece.

TENNESSEE WALTZ

Words & Music: Redd Stewart & Pee Wee King

8

THREE NEW NOTES FOR RIGHT HAND

ISN'T SHE LOVELY

Words & Music: Stevie Wonder

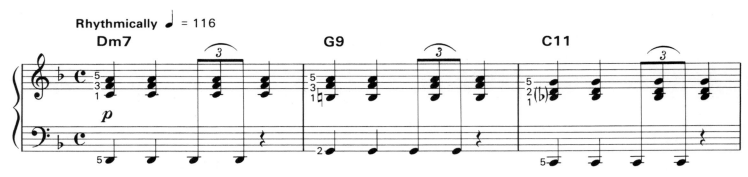

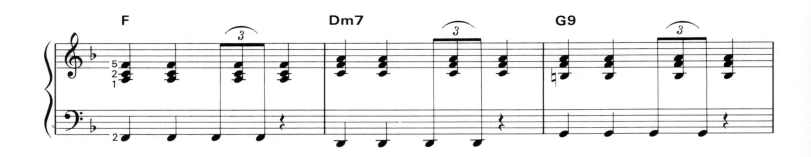

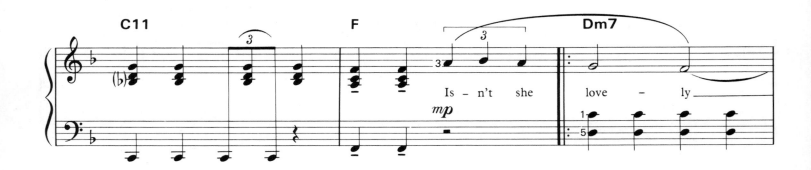

Is – n't she love – ly ____

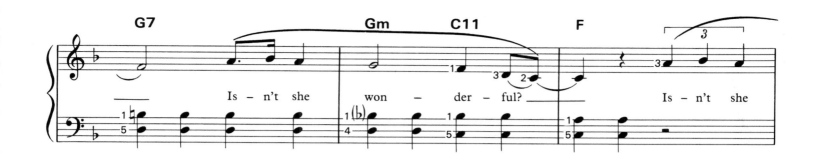

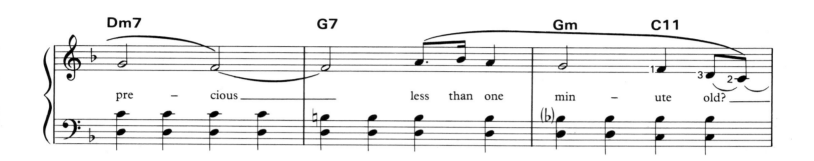

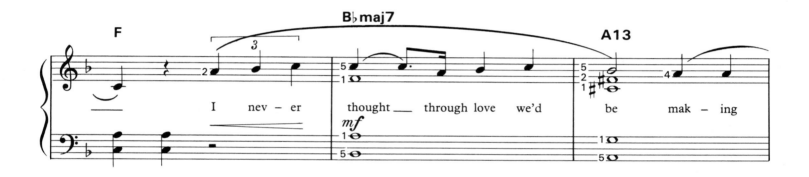

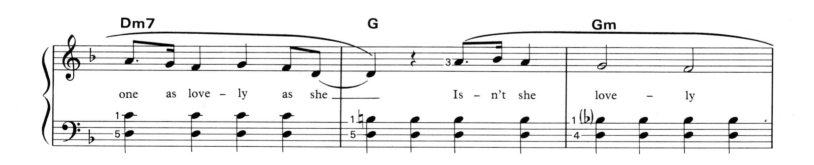

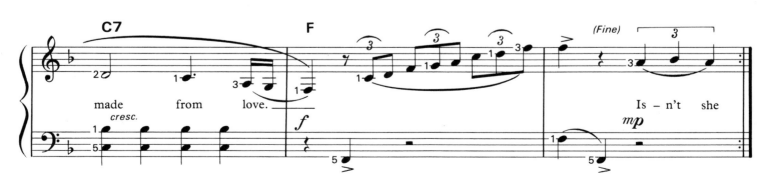

Look out for the new right hand notes in the following piece.

IF I EVER LOSE MY FAITH IN YOU

Words & Music: Sting

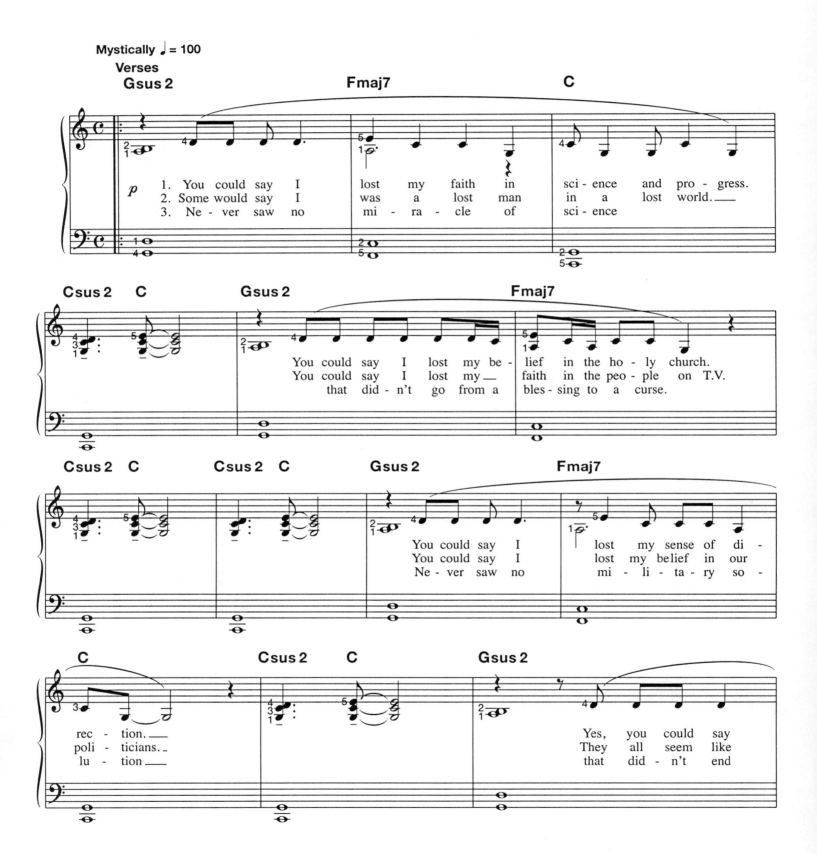

THE PEDALS ON THE PIANO

3

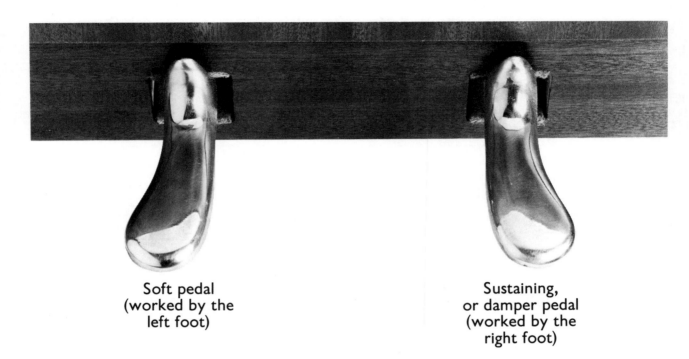

Soft pedal
(worked by the
left foot)

Sustaining,
or damper pedal
(worked by the
right foot)

Soft Pedal
This pedal produces a softer, lighter tone than usual. It is usually indicated in music by the words 'una corda'.

Sustaining, or damper pedal
This pedal lifts the dampers from the strings. This causes the notes played to ring on after the fingers have been lifted from the keys.

The sustaining pedal is the more important of the two pedals. There are several ways of indicating its use. The method we shall use for the moment is:

meaning: pedal down   (hold pedal down)   pedal up

meaning: pedal down   (hold pedal down)   change pedal   (hold pedal down)

(i.e. lift fully then press down again immediately)

The sustaining pedal has two main functions:

1. To combine the notes of a chord:

pedal down   (hold pedal down throughout)   pedal up

2. To link notes in cases where it would be impossible to do so using the fingers alone:

Left hand only

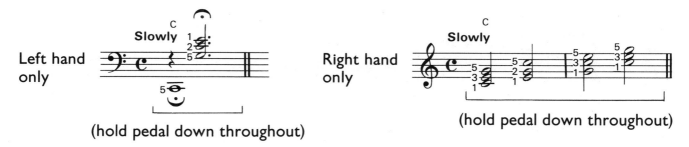

(hold pedal down throughout)

Right hand only

(hold pedal down throughout)

When the harmonies of a piece change it is usual to change the sustaining pedal also:

Left hand only

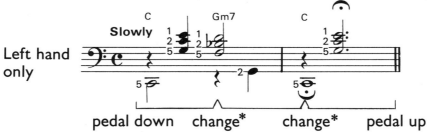

pedal down   change*   change*   pedal up

*(lift as new chord is played, then press down again immediately)

Right hand only

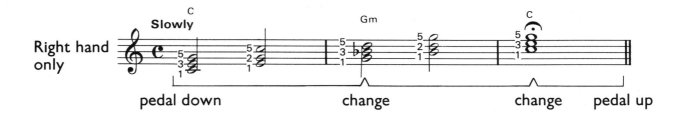

pedal down   change   change   pedal up

PEDAL CHANGING EXERCISE

Using **second finger only**, plus pedal, play the scale below so that it sounds completely 'legato' (joined up).

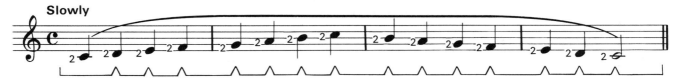

Practise this exercise until you can perform perfect pedal changes.

Here now are four pieces which will give you practice in using the sustaining pedal. Practise each piece first without the pedal. Add the pedal as you become more familiar with the notes. Observe all pedal markings carefully. When making a pedal 'change' note that as the fingers go 'down' (on the new note(s)) the pedal comes 'up'. (It will then go immediately down again).

SCARBOROUGH FAIR

Traditional

THE SOUND OF SILENCE

Words & Music: Paul Simon

*Although the harmony here does not require a change of pedal, the melody does.

BROKEN CHORD STYLE FOR LEFT HAND

In this style the left hand provides a nice flowing accompaniment by moving up and down the notes of the chord. The style is greatly enhanced by the use of the sustaining pedal, since this causes the single notes to build into full chords.

This style is different from the 'arpeggio (broken chord) style' for left hand, first used in Book Three, p.22. In that earlier style the left hand simply split the notes of the chord rapidly upwards, and involved no specific timing. Here there is a rhythm pattern present.

MY WAY
Words: Paul Anka. Music: Claude Francois & Jacques Revaux

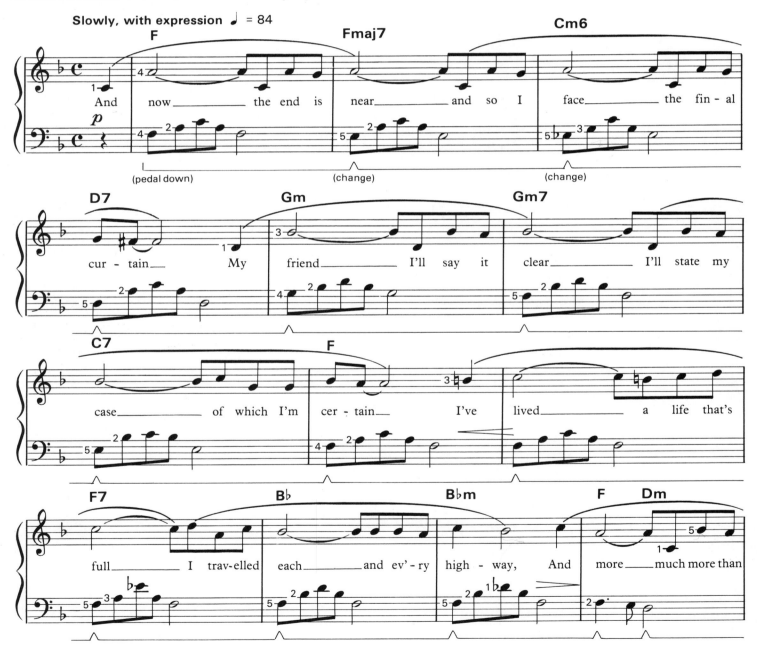

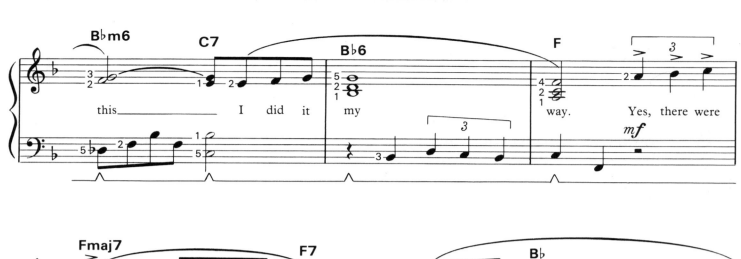

this _____ I did it my way. Yes, there were

times _____ I'm sure you knew _____ when I bit off more than I could

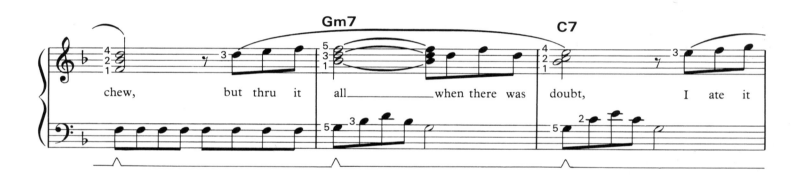

chew, but thru it all _____ when there was doubt, I ate it

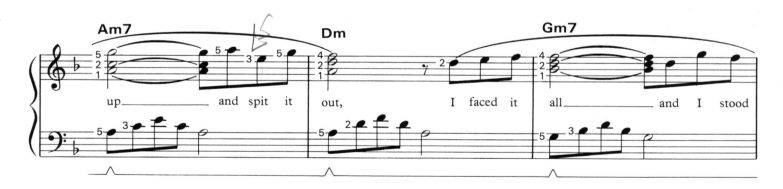

up _____ and spit it out, I faced it all _____ and I stood

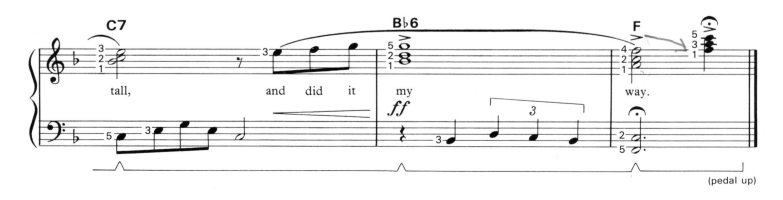

tall, and did it my way.

(pedal up)

Before playing the next piece turn back
to Book Three, p.16, and read about
⁶⁄₈ Time again.

(THEME FROM) **VIOLIN CONCERTO** (SLOW MOVEMENT)

By Felix Mendelssohn

*Semiquaver rest (a silence equal to the value of one semiquaver).

(pedal up)

5

The 'Key of B flat (major)' is derived from the 'Scale of B flat (major)', which requires two black notes: B flat and E flat:

Scale of B♭

Ⓑ♭ C D Ⓔ♭ F G A Ⓑ♭

Pieces using this scale predominantly are said to be in the 'key of B flat'.

The 'Key signature' for the Key of B♭ is:—

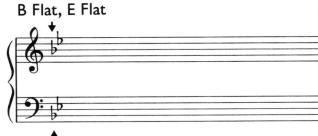

Key of B♭

B Flat, E Flat

B Flat, E Flat

When you are in this Key you must remember to play all B's and E's (wherever they might fall on the keyboard) as B flats and E flats.

THE FOOL ON THE HILL

Words & Music: John Lennon and Paul McCartney

Con moto (with movement) ♩ = 108

B♭maj7   Cm7

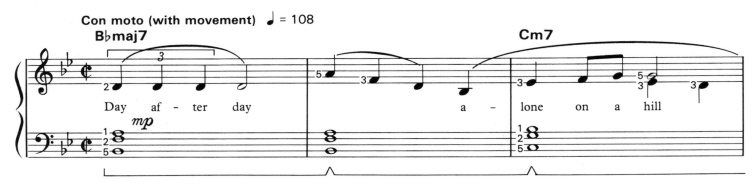

Day af - ter day   *mp*   a - lone on a hill

F7   B♭maj7   B♭6

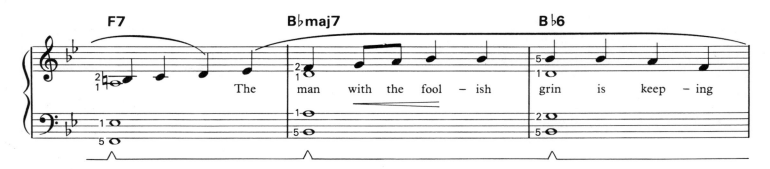

The man with the fool - ish grin is keep - ing

Cm7   F7   Cm7

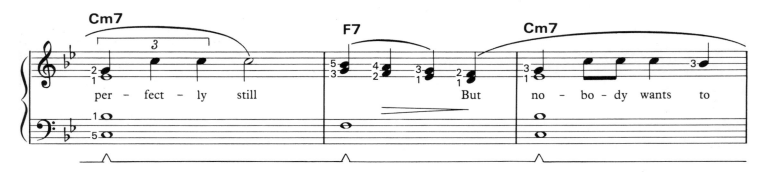

per - fect - ly still   But   no - bo - dy wants to

VERSE AND CHORUS

6

Mockin' Bird Hill is divided into two main sections: the 'verse' and the 'chorus'. The Verse section of a song usually contains the bulk of the narrative and is sung by a solo singer. The Chorus (the main and usually the best known section of a song) is the part where the audience joins in.

You will get a crisper effect from this piece if you do not use the sustaining pedal.

Before you play *Mockin' Bird Hill* turn back to Book Three, p.18, and re-read about 'two-note slurs'.

MOCKIN' BIRD HILL
Words & Music: Vaughn Horton

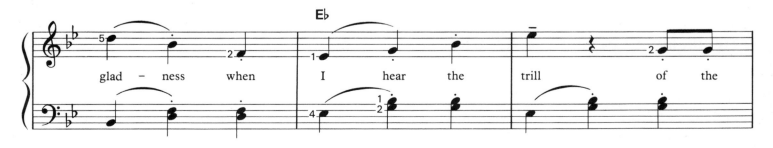

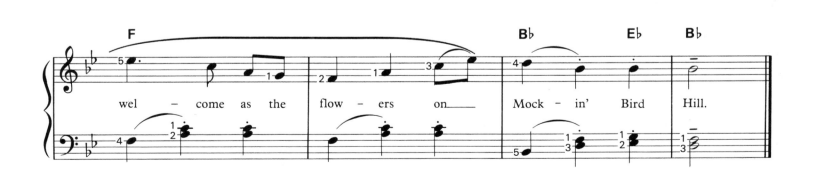

SYNCOPATION

7

When an important, accented note is played just before, or just after a main beat, rather than on it, the effect is called 'syncopation'.

For example:

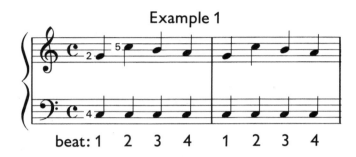

Example 1

beat: 1 2 3 4 1 2 3 4

No syncopation (each melody note is played on a main beat).

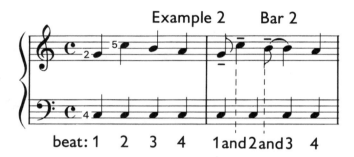

Example 2   Bar 2

beat: 1 2 3 4 1 and 2 and 3 4

Syncopation in Bar 2 (Melody notes 'C' and 'B' play **in between** main beats).

Play the second example through several times. The repeated left hand 'C's' will give you the main beats. Keep the left hand rock-steady throughout.

The above is a simplified version of the start of *Peacherine Rag*. Here now are these same two bars as you will actually play them:

Play Example 3 through many times to get the feel of the syncopation. Keep the left hand rock-steady and play the right hand melody notes with, and in between, the left hand notes as required.

Example 3 Peacherine Rag

beat: 1 2 3 4 1 and 2 and 3 and 4 and

PEACHERINE RAG

By Scott Joplin

Here's a famous modern piece which uses syncopation: *The Fifty-Ninth Street Bridge Song*, by Paul Simon.

Notice the Swing-style 'dotted rhythms' (see Book Three, p.46) which help give the piece a nice lilt.

I have arrowed the first seven syncopated notes for you. Try to find the others for yourself (there are eighteen more). As in *'Peacherine Rag'*, keep your left hand rock-steady throughout.

THE FIFTY-NINTH STREET BRIDGE SONG
(FEELIN' GROOVY)

Words & Music: Paul Simon

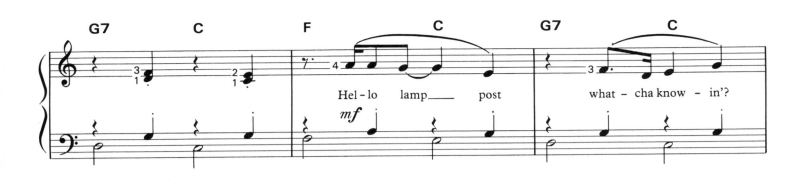

Hel - lo lamp____ post what - cha know - in'?

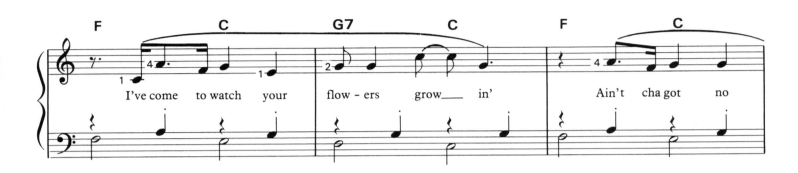

I've come to watch your flow - ers grow____ in' Ain't cha got no

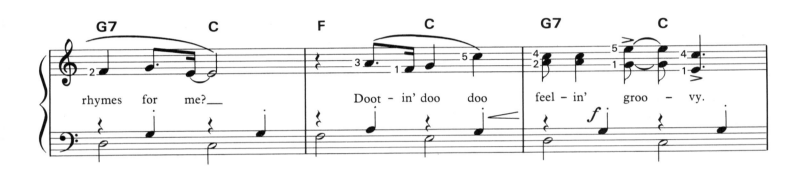

rhymes for me?___ Doot - in' doo doo feel - in' groo - vy.

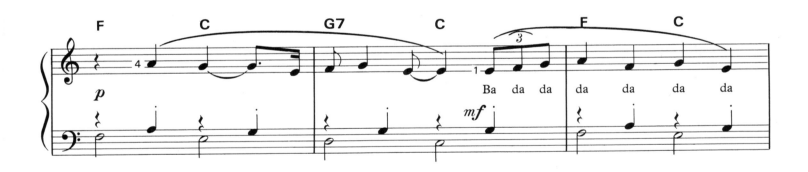

Ba da da da da da da

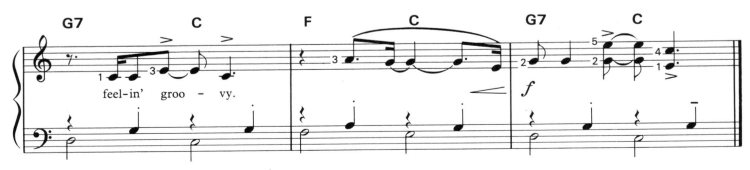

feel-in' groo - vy.

Latin American style tunes use syncopation too, as can be seen in this charming Bossa Nova* called 'Little Boat'.

Since the left hand does not play on every beat in this piece you will have to maintain a strong rhythm in your head!

O BARQUINHO (LITTLE BOAT)

Music: Roberto Menescal. Original Words: Ronaldo Boscoli. English Lyric: Buddy Kaye

*A Latin-American dance rhythm.

In *Pushbike Song* both left and right hands have syncopated notes (I have arrowed the left hand ones for you). When the left hand is not actually laying down the beats (e.g. Bars 9-16) you will have to maintain the time mentally (nod your head strongly on every beat in the early stages of practice).

THE PUSHBIKE SONG

Words & Music: Idris & Evan Jones

*Sforzando. Strongly emphasised.

KEY OF D

8

The 'Key of D (major)' is derived from the 'Scale of D (major)', which requires two black notes: F sharp and C sharp:

Scale of D

D E (F#) G A B (C#) D

The Key signature is therefore:

Key of D

F sharp, C sharp

F sharp, C sharp

When you are in this Key you must remember to play all F's and C's (wherever they might fall on the keyboard) as F sharps and C sharps.

Notice the Left Hand accompaniment 'patterns' in the chorus of the following piece.

DON'T CRY FOR ME ARGENTINA
Music: Andrew Lloyd Webber. Lyrics: Tim Rice

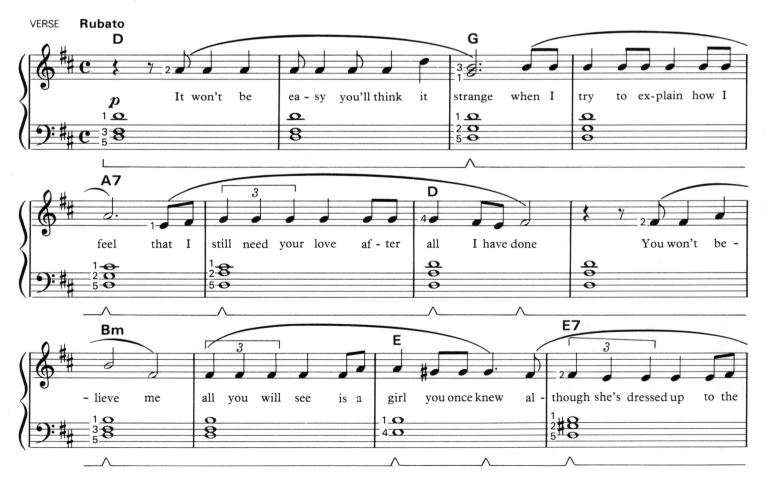

VERSE **Rubato**

It won't be ea-sy you'll think it strange when I try to ex-plain how I

feel that I still need your love af-ter all I have done You won't be-

-lieve me all you will see is a girl you once knew al-though she's dressed up to the

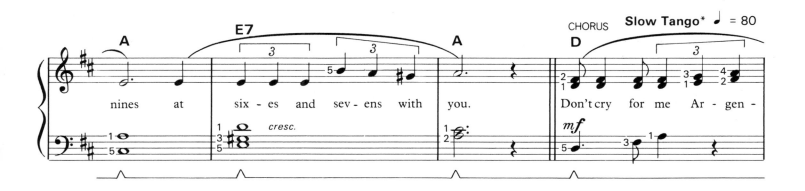

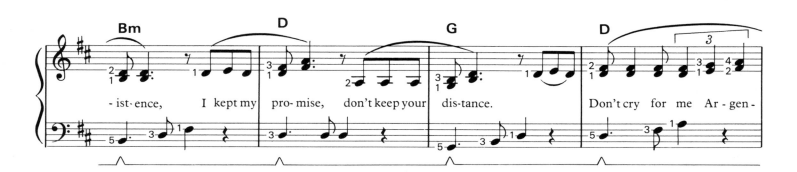

*A popular dance rhythm of African and
Latin-American origin.

KEY OF D MINOR

9

The Key of D Minor is derived from the Scale of D Minor, which requires one black note: B flat:

Scale of D Minor (Natural)

D   E   F   G   A   (Bb)   C   D

The key signature is therefore:

Key of D Minor

B flat

This is the same key signature as F Major:–

Key of F (Major)

B flat

Since they share the same key signature, these two keys are said to be 'related':

D Minor is the Relative Minor of F Major

F Major is the Relative Major of D Minor

Quite often in the key of D Minor you will come across a C 'sharp' or a B 'natural'. Neither of these notes appears in the scale given above. These variations occur because there are two other types of D Minor scale in common use which actually use C sharp and B natural:

Scale of D Minor (Harmonic)

D   E   F   G   A   (Bb)   (C#)   D

Scale of D Minor (Melodic)

D   E   F   G   A   (B)   (C#)   D

When in the key of D Minor remember:

1. You must play all B's (wherever they might fall on the keyboard) as B flats.

2. Look out for occasional C sharps and B naturals (they will be marked as they occur).

OCTAVES IN THE RIGHT HAND

10

This is a most important piano technique which will make your playing sound fuller and more professional.

First practise playing a scale (the scale of C will do) with your right hand to get the feeling of 'octaves' (a distance of eight notes):

Scale of C (Repeat ad lib)

Try other scales similarly.

Next go over some of the easier pieces in the previous books, playing your right hand in octaves throughout.

Note: if the size of your hand allows, finger all black note octaves: $\frac{4}{1}$ rather than: $\frac{5}{1}$. This makes for smoother playing.

The next piece: *'The Green Leaves Of Summer'* is in the key of D Minor.

In the first part your left hand will be using a technique which you have seen before: 'chord pyramids' (see Book Three, p.6).

In the second part your right hand will play the melody in 'octaves'. Since this involves jumping about you will need to use the sustaining pedal to make this section sound 'legato'.

THE GREEN LEAVES OF SUMMER

Words: Paul Francis Webster. Music: Dimitri Tiomkin

Hava Nagila' (in the key of D minor) will give you further practice in right hand octaves.

If you have a large hand, finger the 'black note' octaves $\frac{4}{1}$: if not you will have to finger all octaves $\frac{5}{1}$.

HAVA NAGILA
Traditional

KEY OF E MINOR

E Minor is the 'Relative Minor' of G Major,
both keys requiring one sharp: F sharp:

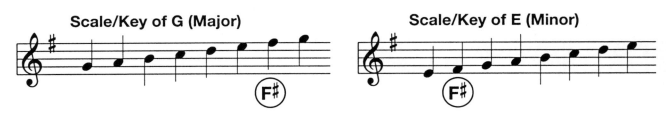

The 'accidentals'* likely to occur in the key of
E Minor (due to other forms of the E Minor
Scale) are: **D♯ and C♯**

A TASTE OF HONEY

Words: Ric Marlow. Music: Bobby Scott

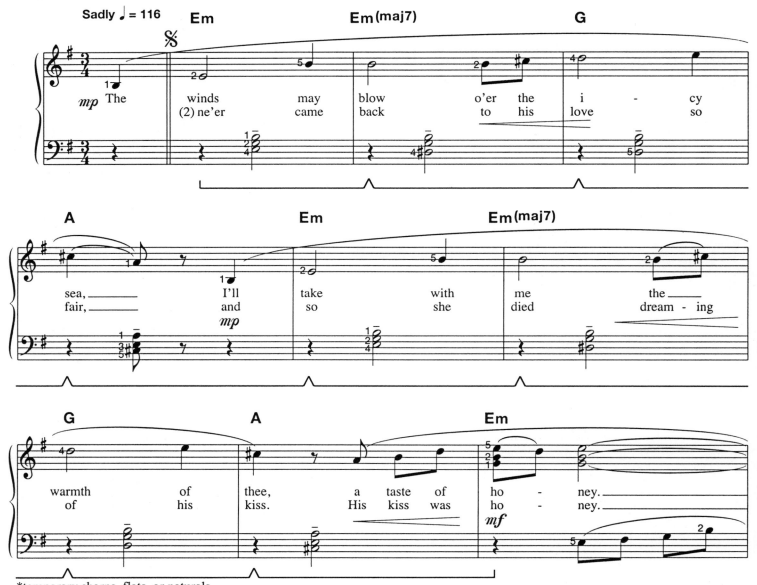

*temporary sharps, flats, or naturals.

ALTERNATIVE PEDAL MARKING

12 An alternative and simpler method of indicating the sustaining pedal will be used from now on:

P means 'apply' or 'change' the pedal, the equivalent of: ⌐_____ or:_____⌃
⋆ means 'lift' the Pedal.

LEFT HAND FILLS

13 In *'Laura'* your left hand will be playing 'fills' or 'fill-ins'. These are short melodic fragments which fill in the 'dead spots' in the right hand part and help keep the piece moving. Play all your fills 'legato' and with expression.

LAURA
Words: Johnny Mercer. Music: David Raksin

43

BOSSA NOVA RHYTHM PATTERN

14

In the next piece you play a simple, but effective Bossa Nova rhythm pattern in your left hand:

The pattern begins in Bar 5 and continues through most of the first part of the song.

count: 1   2 and 3   4

JUST THE WAY YOU ARE
Words & Music: Billy Joel

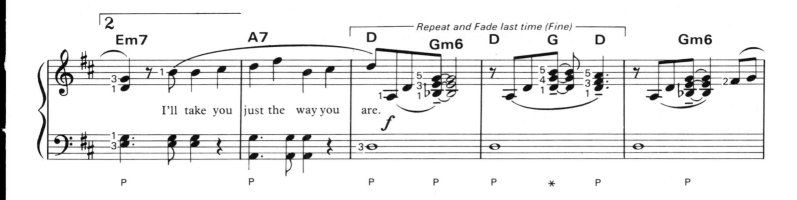

I'll take you just the way you are.

I need to know that you will al - ways be

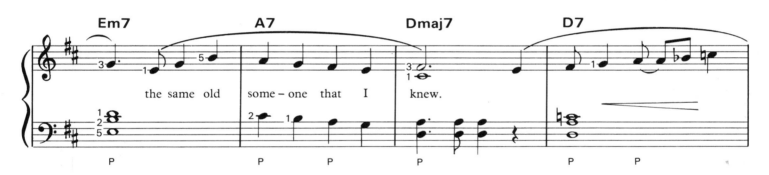

the same old some - one that I knew.

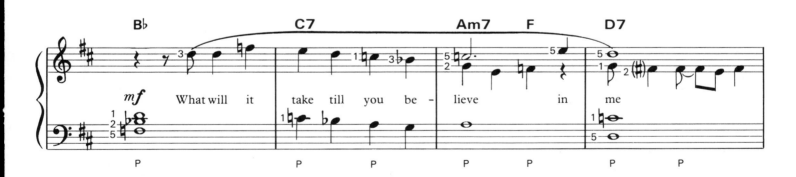

What will it take till you be - lieve in me the way that

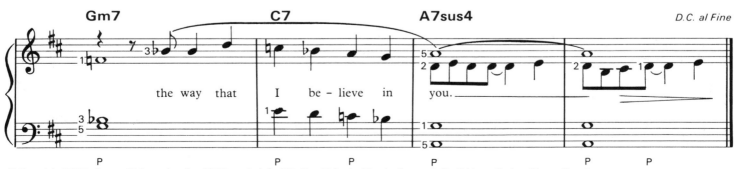

the way that I be - lieve in you.

KEY OF G MINOR

15

G Minor is the 'Relative Minor' of B flat Major, both keys requiring two flats: B flat and E flat:

Scale/Key of B♭ (Major)

Ⓑ♭   Ⓔ♭   Ⓑ♭

The accidentals likely to occur in the Key of G Minor are: F♯ and E♮

Scale/Key of G Minor

Ⓑ♭   Ⓔ♭

The following piece begins in the key of G Minor and modulates (i.e. changes key) in the last section to B♭ Major.

(THEME FROM) SYMPHONY NO. 40
By W.A. Mozart

46

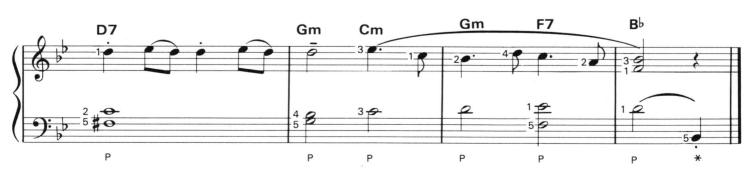

LAST WORD

Congratulations on reaching the end of Book Four of 'The Complete Piano Player'.

In Book Five You will be:
- Playing in $\frac{12}{8}$ time
- Playing in more new keys
- Adding left hand octaves
- Improving your phrasing
- Learning exciting new modern styles.

Till then your last song in this book is:

THANK YOU FOR THE MUSIC

Words & Music: Benny Andersson & Bjorn Ulvaeus

8/99 (34923)